# Circus
## Coloring Book

Aryla Publishing 2020

978-1-912675-83-8

www.arylapublishing.com

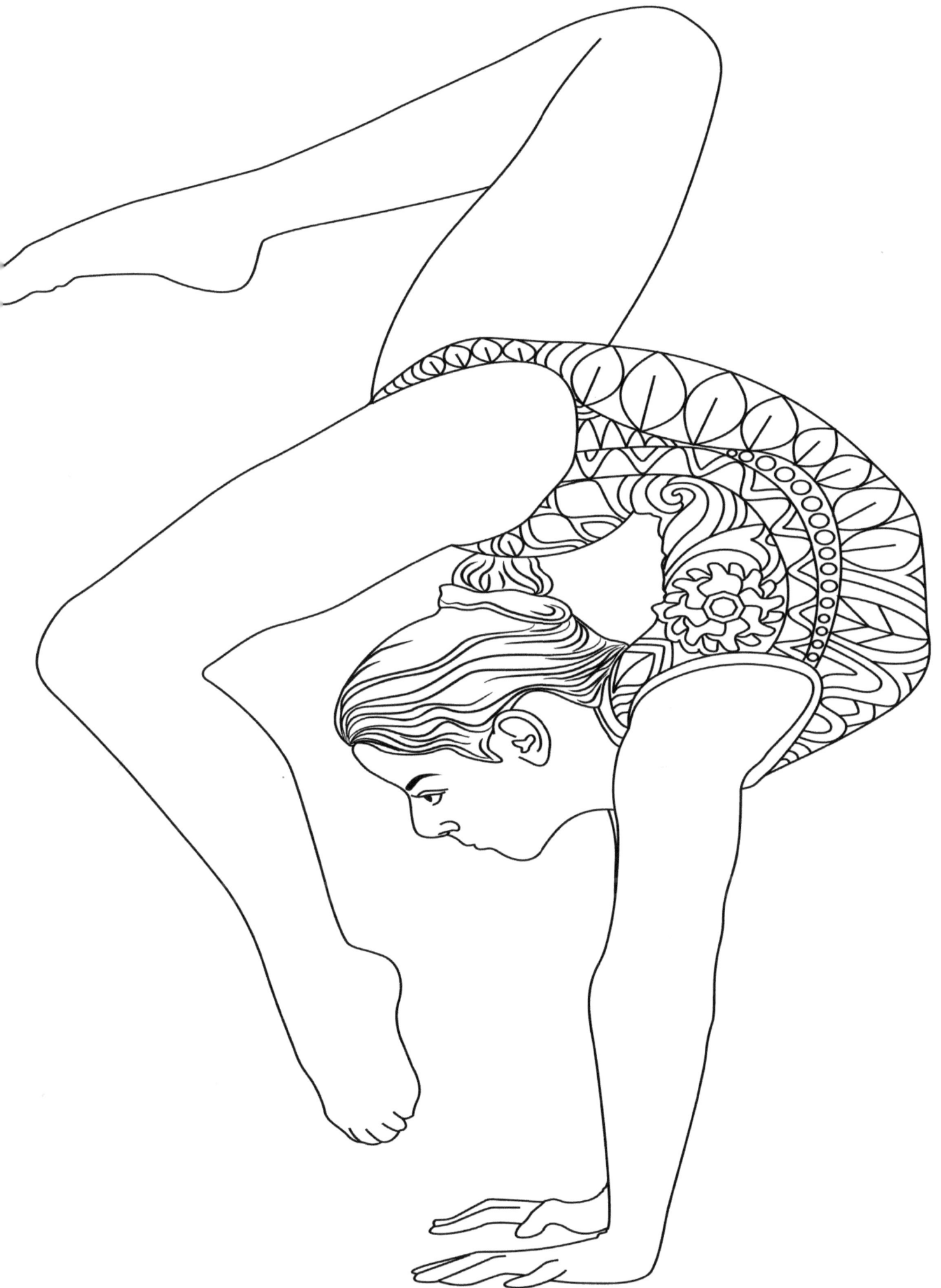

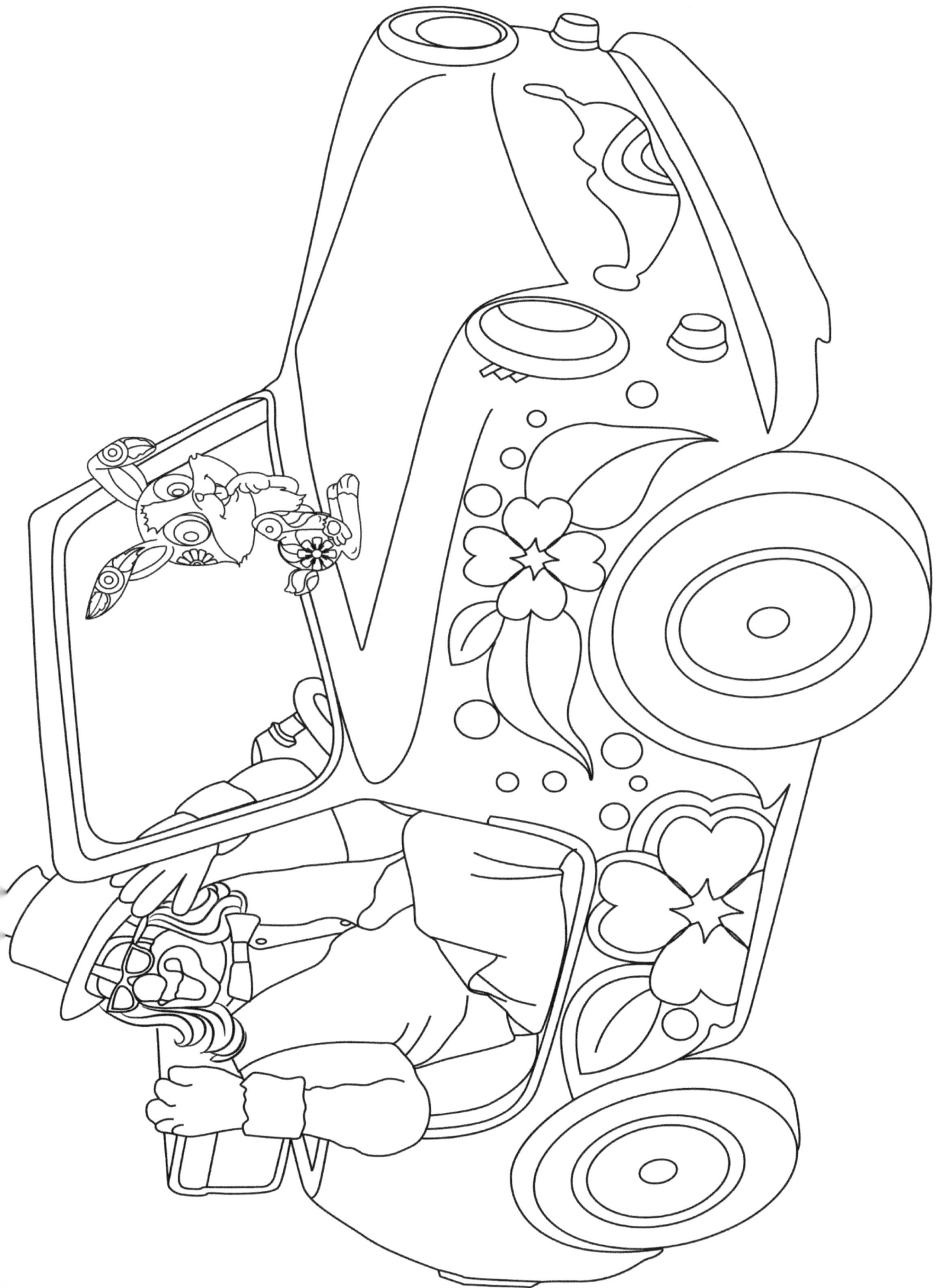

Thank you for purchasing this book.

If you would like to know more about Aryla Publishing Books please visit:-

**www.ArylaPublishing.com**

Or follow us on
**Facebook**
**Twitter**
**Instagram**
for *free promotions*

**@arylapublishing**

We would love to know what you think of this book so please leave us a review.

Have a wonderful day ☺

# Other Coloring Books from Aryla Publishing

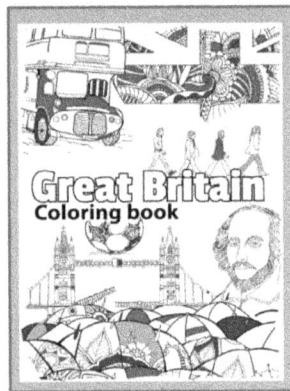

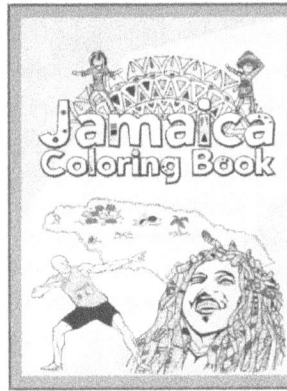

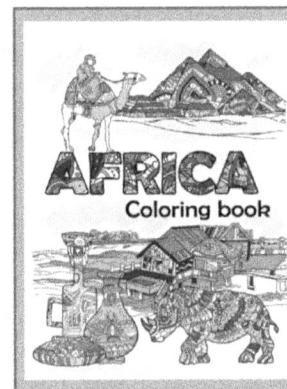

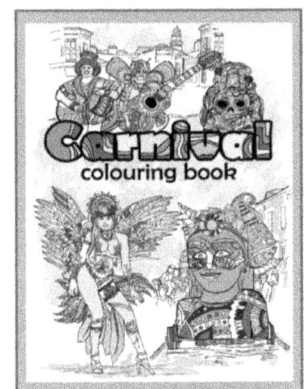

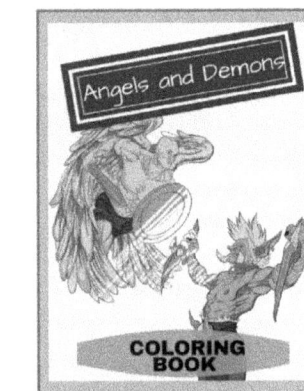

Great Britain Coloring book

U.S.A. Coloring book

Jamaica Coloring Book

Mexico Coloring book

PIRATE Coloring Book

DRAGON Coloring Book

UNICORN Coloring Book

MERMAIDS Coloring Book

Black Inventors Coloring Book

Spain Coloring book

AFRICA Coloring book

Carnival colouring book

1920'S COLORING BOOK

Kittens and Puppies COLORING BOOK

Black Brothers COLORING BOOK

Angels and Demons COLORING BOOK

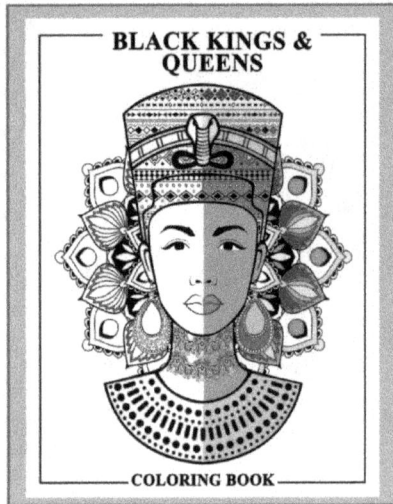

BLACK KINGS & QUEENS

COLORING BOOK

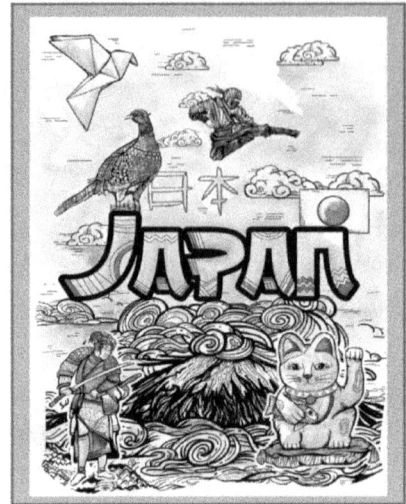

JAPAN

BLACK HEROES

Coloring Book

ANIMAL COLORING BOOK

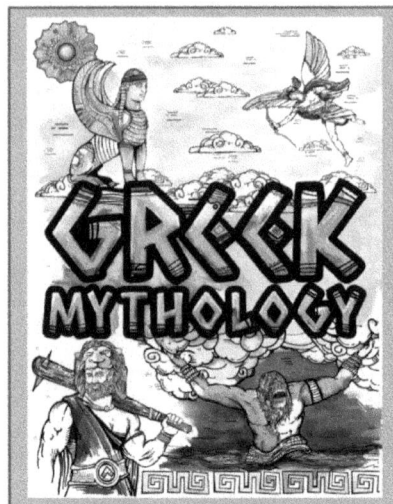

GREEK MYTHOLOGY

# Color In Fun
# Kids Books

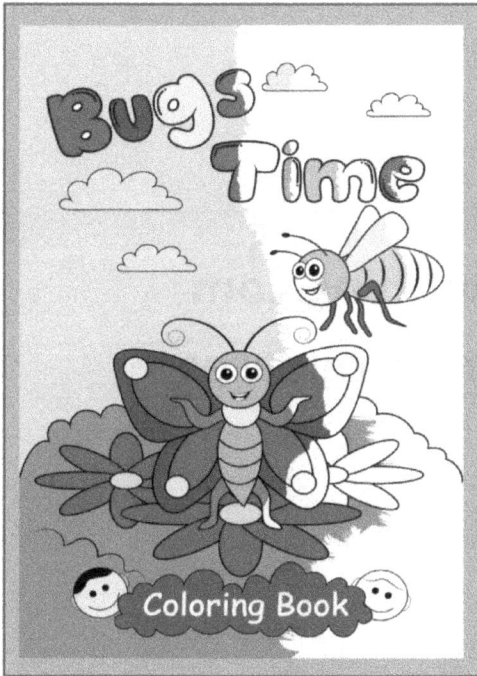

Bugs Time — Coloring Book

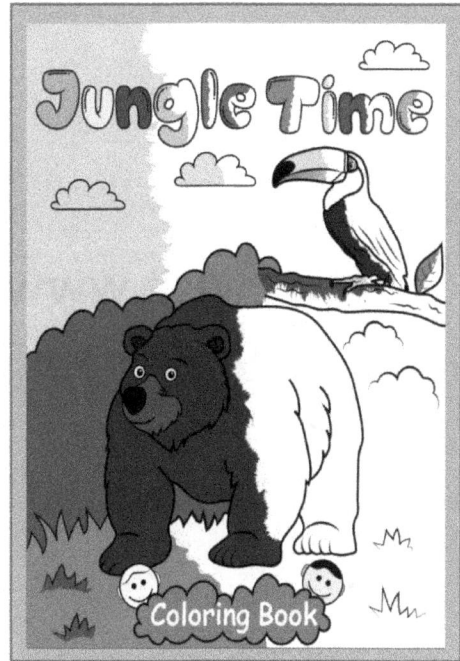

Jungle Time — Coloring Book

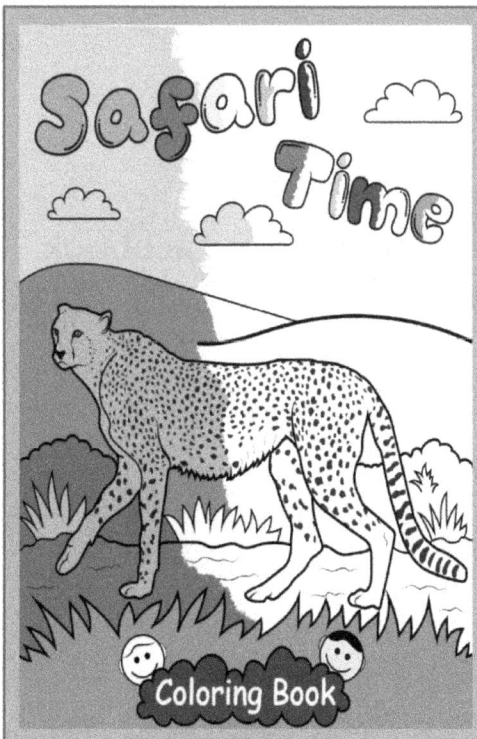

Safari Time — Coloring Book

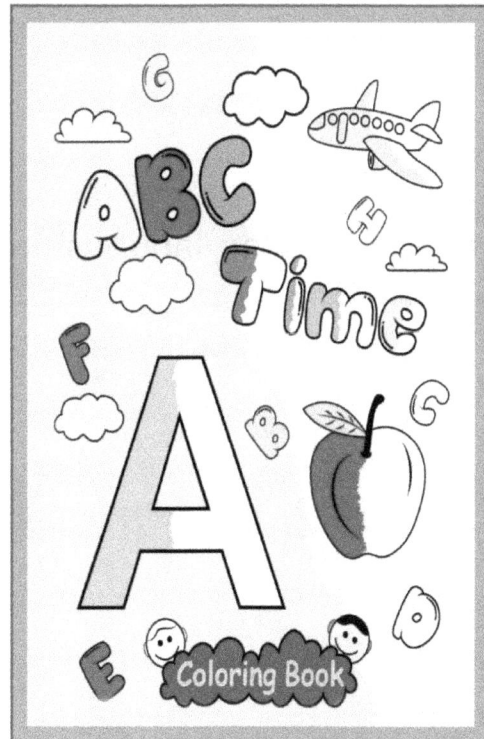

ABC Time — Coloring Book

Visit **www.ArylaPublishing.com**
to find out about all new releases.

Follow us @arylapublishing on Twitter Instagram & Facebook

Search for Aryla Publishing on

**YouTube**

**Check out our Book Trailers**

**Subscribe to keep up to date with new releases!**

# WE WOULD LOVE YOUR FEEDBACK

## PLEASE LEAVE REVIEW AT:-

www.ingramcontent.com/pod-product-compliance
Lightning Source LLC
Chambersburg PA
CBHW081222020426

42331CB00012B/3075